D1576957

WILDLIFE OF
SCOTLAND

Colin Baxter Photography, Grantown-on-Spey, Scotland

WILDLIFE OF SCOTLAND

Scotland is admired around the world for its rugged and unspoiled beauty. It is predominantly a country of hills, lochs, seas and islands. Within its 7.8 million hectares it has 90% of the UK's wild upland habitats, over 27,000 lochs representing 91% of the volume of the UK's freshwaters, 50,000 kilometres of river and 11,800 kilometres of coast.

Within the rich variety of habitats found in Scotland, there exists a corresponding diversity of wildlife. Each year over 300 species of birds are recorded. Scotland lies on two major migration routes: one from the north from Greenland, Scandinavia and Russia, and the other brings birds from the south from Africa and the Mediterranean.

There are also over 60 species of mammals living wild on land or in the sea, including a host of seals, whales, dolphins and porpoises in our coastal waters. The many less recognised species of migratory fish, reptiles and amphibians here also add greatly to the abundance of wildlife, as too do our exquisite range of plants, from tiny wildflowers to ancient pine forests.

The health of Scotland's natural environment and wildlife rests in a fragile balance, but much is being done by individuals and organisations to conserve it. Be it large or small, on land, in the air or on the water, the wildlife of Scotland is a wonder for everyone to seek out and enjoy, and to preserve for the future.

◀ GOLDEN EAGLE

The golden eagle (*Aquila chrysaetos*) once widespread in the British Isles, is now virtually confined to the mountainous areas of Scotland, with one breeding pair in the north of England. In flight, the golden eagle gives the impression of unequalled power and control, with a wingspan exceeding two metres. Most golden eagles breed on remote cliffs building huge nests of sticks and moss. The Scottish population now consists of over 400 breeding pairs, 20 percent of the total European population.

SCOTTISH WILDCAT

The Scottish wildcat (*Felis sylvestris*) is an elusive creature of wood and moorland with its small UK population now confined to Scotland. Solitary and territorial, these supreme predators lie in wait for their prey, hunting by stealth and surprise rather than by speed. Interbreeding with feral domestic cats is a serious threat to the future of the wildcat.

CORNCRAKE

The rasping call of the corncrake (*Crex crex*) was once familiar over much of lowland Britain. Nesting in hay meadows, corncrakes suffered from increasing farm mechanisation. Today, the UK population is found only in the Hebrides and Orkney, where conservation measures appear to have halted years of decline.

ATLANTIC PUFFIN ▶

The Atlantic puffin (*Fratercula arctica*) is one of Scotland's most attractive and popular birds, well known for its multi-coloured beak, thick black and white plumage and bright orange legs and feet. Puffins are small, not much larger than a pint-sized milk carton and can be found along the shorelines of some Scottish islands and along the far north coast. They feed on fish, particularly sand eels, and are expert swimmers and divers. Scotland is home to about 90 per cent of the UK population.

◄ CAPERCAILLIE

The capercaillie (*Tetrao urogallus*) lives
in dense pinewoods and feeds on pine
shoots, berries and insects. It was thought
to have become extinct in the eighteenth
century, but was reintroduced shortly
afterwards. Once again there is concern
about declining numbers with only about
1,000 capercaillie left in Scotland, which
represents the entire UK population.

CRESTED TIT ►

The crested tit (*Parus cristatus*) is
confined to the Scottish Highlands, where
its distinctive crest marks it out. Time
spent in a Scots pinewood is made special
by the sight and sound of this little bird
as it gathers and stores seeds from pine
cones. There are probably fewer than
a thousand pairs left in Scotland.

◄ SEA EAGLE

The sea eagle or white-tailed eagle (*Haliaeetus albicilla*) is Scotland's largest bird of prey. They live on remote craggy coastlines and rocky islands swooping into sea lochs to take fish, although they prefer hares, rabbits and seabirds. Reintroduced to Scotland in 1975, there are now 25 breeding pairs.

RED SQUIRREL ►

The red squirrel (*Sciurus vulgaris*) prefers to live in coniferous woodland. Travelling fast, they use their bushy tails for balance – its tail is almost as long as its body. They feed on the seeds of pine cones, which they also store for the winter. The red squirrel is Scotland's only native squirrel and there is concern over its future.

PTARMIGAN

The ptarmigan (*Lagopus mutus*) is found in high barren regions of Scotland. It changes colour as camouflage, from mottled grey-brown to almost pure white in winter.

RED FOX ▶

The red fox (*Vulpes vulpes*) adapts well to living in Scotland's varied landscapes, living on a diet of small mammals, birds, insects and carrion supplemented with fruit and berries.

◄ MOUNTAIN HARE

The mountain hare (*Lepus timidus*) is the only native hare left in Britain today. Their population is essentially restricted to Scotland, where they live in open moorland at high altitudes. In mountain habitats they are an important food source for golden eagles, although their coats, which turn white in winter, offer superb camouflage.

WILD GOAT ►

Herds of feral goats (*Capra hircus*) have resulted from accidental or deliberate release of domestic goats over many hundreds of years. They live in small groups, led by a dominant billy goat. Resident in a few hilly and coastal areas of Scotland they feed on all types of vegetation. Scotland has a population of around 2,500.

◀ GREAT SPOTTED WOODPECKER

The great spotted woodpecker (*Dendrocopus major*) is an agile climber with a strong pointed beak and protrudable tongue. They became extinct during the nineteenth century, but re-established themselves in the first half of the twentieth century and are now widely distributed in wooded areas, particularly birch.

PINE MARTEN ▶

The pine marten (*Martes martes*) is thought to be Scotland's rarest native mammal species and may be extinct in England and Wales. Persecuted by man, they are now recovering and re-colonising their former habitats. The distribution of breeding pine martens is confined to areas of tree cover, providing protection from natural predators such as eagles and foxes.

BOTTLENOSE DOLPHIN

Bottlenose dolphins (*Tursiops truncatus*) seen here in the Moray Firth, are relatively uncommon in UK waters. These social animals are quick learners with good memories.

MINKE WHALE ▶

Minke whale (*Balaenoptera acutostrata*) are a familiar sight in the waters of the Hebrides, but are relatively small compared to other whales that visit these waters.

◀ OTTER

The otter (*Lutra lutra*) is a wanderer by nature and needs a large territory for its home range. Otters live along undisturbed and remote stretches of seashore, or in the quieter areas of large rivers, feeding mainly on fish, although they will eat small birds, mammals and amphibians. There are thought to be about 6,500 wild otters in Scotland and the largest dog otters can measure up to 1.2 metres in length and weigh up to 13.5 kilograms. Ever popular, the once endangered otter now thrives in Scotland.

ATLANTIC SALMON

The Atlantic salmon (*Salmo salar*) migrates from the sea into Scotland's rivers to spawn, displaying remarkable accuracy in returning to their home rivers. Some have been known to swim over 160 km up river to the place of their birth, encountering many obstacles on their journey. Up to 95% of salmon then die after spawning.

The osprey (*Pandion haliaetos*) specialises in catching fish, its Gaelic name, *lasgair*, means fisherman. They live and hunt in saltwater and freshwater habitats and have been known to nest on rocks, islets, and typically, in trees. Like many of Scotland's birds of prey, the osprey suffered many centuries of persecution and habitat loss and became extinct in 1916. They returned to Scotland in 1954 and are now protected by law. More osprey's are returning each year, with the current breeding population at 150 pairs.

BLACK GROUSE

In Scotland, the black grouse (*Tetrao tetrix*) is most at home in native Caledonian pine forests, where they nest and feed in heather and bilberry. Black grouse are noted for their communal courtship display known as 'lekking'. The males congregate at traditional lek grounds to perform elaborate displays of calls and dances to attract the females.

◄ REINDEER

Herds of reindeer (*Rangifer tarandus*) would have been common in Scotland some 200,000 years ago. However, the species died out by the end of the twelfth century and today's small herd, managed and maintained in the Cairngorms, is the result of a reintroduction in 1952. Reindeer are suited to Arctic conditions with a thick coat and wide-splayed hooves, which prevent them sinking into snow. They feed primarily on reindeer moss, a type of lichen, and have a rut in September and October, with calves born in May or June.

OYSTERCATCHER

Oystercatchers (*Haematopus ostralegus*), with their striking plumage, are one of Scotland's most distinctive birds and their clamorous 'piping' groups add to the thrill of bird-watching on the coast. The oystercatcher has spread inland since the late 19th century, mainly along rivers and have become a welcome sight on farmland, and by roads.

Buzzard

More common and smaller than the golden eagle, buzzards (*Buteo buteo*) are widespread in Scotland and can be found from heavily wooded areas and farmland to hilly and mountainous areas. They feed on rabbits, small mammals, carrion and a wide variety of birds, reptiles and amphibians. They are often seen in small groups soaring on thermals.

Red Grouse ▶

The red grouse (*Lagopus lagopus scoticus*) is a subspecies of the willow ptarmigan. In Britain much of its habitat is centred on moorland where it nests, feeds and hides from predators in the heather. It is a secretive bird, flying low over the ground when it is disturbed before landing a few hundred metres away. On some moors where numbers are kept artificially high for shooting, phenomenal densities of over 600 birds per kilometre square have been recorded.

BLACK-THROATED DIVER AND RED-THROATED DIVER

The black-throated diver (*Gavia artica*), left, and red-throated diver (*Gavia stellata*), above, are typical features of the wild, wet moors of the north and west of Scotland and some Scottish islands. They nest in lochans and pools and feed at sea or in larger lochs.

COMMON SEAL

The common seal (*Phoca vitulina*) is found around Scotland's coasts, feeding on small fish and shellfish and frequently seen sunbathing on rocks or sandbanks. Common seal pups are born in summer, whilst grey seal pups are born during autumn and winter.

GREY SEAL PUP ▶

GANNET

Photographs © 2003: Colin Baxter: 7, 12, 14, 19, 30, 31, 32
Laurie Campbell: front cover, 1, 4, 5, 10, 11, 13, 16, 17, 18, 20,
21, 22, 27, 28, 29   Mark Hamblin: back cover, 6, 25, 26,
Neil McIntyre: 2, 8, 15, 23, 24   Peter Cairns: 9

Text Copyright © Colin Baxter Photography Ltd 2003

A CIP Catalogue record for this book
is available from the British Library.

ISBN 1-84107-171-4

Colin Baxter Gift Book Series

First published in Great Britain in 2003 by
Colin Baxter Photography Ltd,
Grantown-on-Spey, PH26 3NA, Scotland

www.colinbaxter.co.uk